FROM *me* TO *you*

MARK & SUSAN MERRILL

HARVEST HOUSE PUBLISHERS
EUGENE, OREGON

Cover design by Mary Eakin Design

Interior design by Steve Kuhn Design

From Me to You
Copyright © 2019 Mark and Susan Merrill
Published by Harvest House Publishers
Eugene, Oregon 97408
www.harvesthousepublishers.com

ISBN 978-0-7369-7572-8 (hardcover)

Printed in China

19 20 21 22 23 24 25 26 27 / RDS-SK / 10 9 8 7 6 5 4 3 2 1

Dear Parent...

Do your conversations with your daughter ever seem like a litany of corrections and instructions? Perhaps they sound like this: "Did you brush your teeth?" "Did you feed the dog?" "Please don't provoke your brother!" "Your softball uniform is on the dryer." "When is your next orthodontist appointment?" "How could you forget your homework?" "I told you, you can't wear that to school!"

With school, sports, recitals, holidays, and church programs—in our case, for five children—life can easily spin out of control. Survival became our goal because everyone in the family was moving so fast. Communication became utilitarian, and relationships were sometimes strained.

FROM SUSAN: So many nights I fell into bed and couldn't remember a single meaningful word I said to my kids all day. It started to bother me. I felt as if my only role as a parent was to bark out basic instructions as my family flew by. I craved deeper conversations with my kids. I often dropped them off at school after a rushed morning and drove away wishing I could circle back, pick them up, and look deeply into their eyes until I felt they really saw me. Then I could tell them how much I loved them rather than yelling it out of the window as they scrambled to class.

I felt so guilty. I was missing opportunities to praise and encourage them because I was too busy reminding and instructing. I was pining for more tender moments with them and wanting to share more kind words. In my desire to make sure we got everything done right—including getting to school on time—I was squelching the sweetness and joy God intended for our relationship.

FROM MARK: At the same time, I was experiencing much of what Susan was feeling. I was a "joy squelcher" too. I knew something was missing in the way we were raising our kids but couldn't quite put my finger on it. The busyness of life was blowing away opportunities for Susan and me to encourage our children and go deeper relationally with them. It was time for a change.

God made that clear one morning through an incident with our oldest child, Megan. Susan had been coaching Megan to have more patience with her younger siblings, who adored her but were often annoying to her.

On the way to school on a morning of particularly annoying adoration, Susan observed Megan responding to one of the kids with intentional patience. She then gave Susan the *Do you see me, Mom?* look in the rearview mirror. Susan smiled back with approval, but of course, she couldn't say a word.

FROM SUSAN: We arrived at school, the kids got out of the car, and I drove away, marveling that Megan had put into practice what we had discussed. I so badly wanted to encourage her to continue being patient with her siblings.

Then my joy turned pensive. I began to worry that I would forget to praise her after school. I knew I would be distracted getting all the kids where they needed to be, finishing homework, preparing dinner…you know the drill. But

I was not going to miss this opportunity to encourage her. I drove home and immediately wrote her a long note of praise and left it on her pillow.

Why are indelible words on paper often more powerful than fleeting comments?

Megan found the note on her pillow and did something I will never forget. She wrote me back and put her note on *my* pillow. That night when I dropped into bed, instead of falling asleep craving more connection with my kids, I felt overwhelming gratefulness that God had inspired me to do something so simple.

The next day I started a *From Me to You* journal with each of my kids. I wrote down a question—usually about something going on in their life. Then I wrote my thoughts and words of encouragement. I placed it on the child's pillow and waited for him or her to write back. *From Me to You* gave each of them a comfortable way to express themselves to us and gave us a clear window into their minds and emotions.

FROM MARK: As Susan and the kids wrote words of encouragement to one another, I watched their lines of communication open up and their relationship grow in a huge way. I wanted that same experience. So I grabbed their journals and joined the conversation. We asked meaningful questions instead of giving instructions. We listened instead of lecturing. As a result, we found the connection with our kids we had been craving.

Recently, we pulled out the journals for each of our children. As we opened the pages, we saw the cute drawings, the fun stickers, and their developing handwriting. But what captured our hearts was the evidence of God's hand in their lives. The thoughts they shared about dreams and fears and so much more helped us guide and parent. It made a difference in our relationships and our family.

BENEFITS

From Me to You is a conversation journal you can use to communicate with your daughter and encourage her. It includes fun questions to prompt important conversations that don't normally happen in everyday life. It provides a way for you to share postitive words of encouragement your daughter can read over and over. You'll build a deeper connection with her—and stop feeling guilty for settling for less. You'll learn what your daughter has been thinking on a deeper level. And when this journal is filled, you'll have a keepsake of wonderful memories and her developing thoughts.

4 STEPS TO CONNECT WITH YOUR DAUGHTER USING *FROM ME TO YOU*

 ### *Communicate!*

In our busy and distracted world, communication is getting crushed. We must put down the phone and try to stop, look, listen, and laugh.

- *Stop* your busy day long enough to catch your daughter doing something *right*—and *write* about it in *From Me to You.*

- *Look* at your daughter's life—school, friends, activities, free time—and tune in to what interests her. In *From Me to You*, ask her questions about her interests.

- *Listen* to your daughter's responses. The prompts in this journal will stimulate daily conversations. Whatever your daughter says, listen! Sometimes, seemingly mindless chatter has a hidden agenda. Your daughter may be testing your reaction to something she really wants to tell you, but she may not be sure how you will receive it. Listen rather than react. Your response can open or close your daughter's heart to further conversation.

- *Laugh* with your daughter! Laughter will make *From Me to You* fun and encouraging. Deeper discussions will come as a result of the comfort and trust your daughter feels from sharing silly and humorous moments.

 ## Be Creative!

Using *From Me to You* creatively can deepen a relationship or ease a strained one. Use the ideas below to have fun while growing closer to your daughter. They can also help you entice her if she is hesitant to participate.

- *Draw a picture.* One of our daughters is very artistic and often drew her answer to a prompt. Or she would write a response and then spend a great deal of time embellishing the page. Her journals are beautiful.

- *Use fill-in-the-blanks or check boxes.* If your daughter doesn't love to write, these formats will help her to respond. One of our children did not enjoy writing but was drawn into the fun after laughing at the crazy multiple-choice questions.

- *Insert articles or pictures.* Look online for items about your daughter's favorite athlete, musician, or movie star, or print pictures from your phone of special moments in her life.

Encourage, Encourage, Encourage!

When we started using these journals, our pimary goal was to encourage—to give our children courage. We wanted to fill them with the joy of knowing that we saw beautiful possibilities in them. Make encouraging words and phrases a part of your daily vocabulary, liberally sprinkling them throughout *From Me to You*. If you struggle finding creative, encouraging words to share with your daughter, visit **markmerrill.com/frommetoyou** or **susanme.com/fromme toyou**, where you'll find a list of hundreds of encouraging phrases you can use.

Pursue!

The first time you write in *From Me to You*, choose a question that is relevant to your daughter's life at the moment. Feel free to skip around the journal by bookmarking the question you've written about. Some of the questions apply to both of you, so open up and share. Some of the questions will be for your daughter, so start your note with encouragement. End your note by asking your daughter what she thinks. Place the journal on her pillow.

Some children may hesitate to write back. If you don't receive a response within a few days, try again with a different question. Keep pursuing, encouraging, and sharing your thoughts about the question prompts. Keep incorporating things that interest her. Your daughter loves you and will treasure your words of encouragement, even if she never shows it by writing back. There is no rule for how often you should write. Don't pressure yourself (especially if you are writing to multiple children). Write when you're inspired by all the wonderful things you see in your daughter and enjoy connecting with her!

We are excited about the journey you are about to take into your daughter's heart. The words we have captured in *From Me to You* journals with our children are reflections for which we are eternally grateful. We thank God for the inspiration He gave Susan years ago, which has resulted in pages of precious conversations with all of our kids. Conversations about trials with teachers, friends, coaches. Conversations about temptations and fears. Conversations about dreams, family, and faith.

We will be praying for you and your daughter to experience what we did. Most of all, we will be praying that when you fall into bed at night, your heart will be filled with peace as you ponder the words you and your daughter shared that day.

Lastly, this introduction is just for you, the parent. Tear out these pages, and you are ready to begin!

> With love and hope,
> Susan and Mark Merrill

My best friends are...

and I like them because...

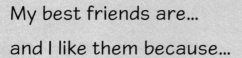

When was the last time someone hurt your feelings?

How did you react?

Parent

Child

What do you think makes you
unique or special?

Parent

Child

You have become very good at...

Parent

Child

Sometimes I wish I could...

Parent

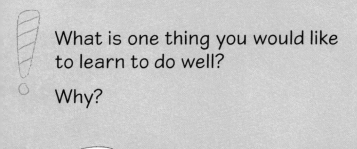

What is one thing you would like
to learn to do well?

Why?

Parent

Three words I would use to
describe you are...

because...

Parent

What is your favorite thing to do,
just the two of us together?

Parent

Child

The thing I would like to do most
with my friends is...

Parent

Child

What is your favorite family tradition?

What tradition would you like to start?

Parent

Child

Who in our family works the hardest around the house?

How can you help them?

Parent

Three words I would use to
describe myself are...

because...

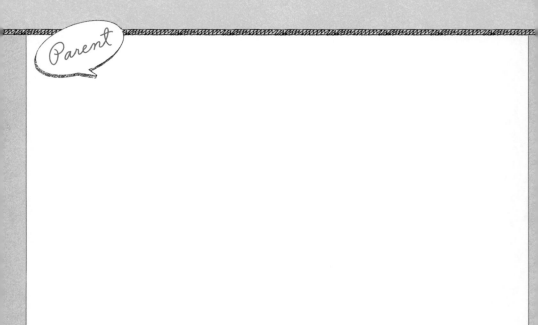

Parent

Child

The thing I love about you the most is...

Parent

Child

If we had ten days to go anywhere in the world together, I would want to go to...

Child

What is your favorite part
of your school day?

Parent

Child

I felt really good when you told me...

Parent

Child

If you could change one thing about yourself,
what would you change?

Parent

Child

If you could ask God one question,
what would you ask?

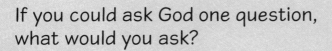
Parent

Child

Of all the things you do for me,
the one I appreciate most is...

because...

Parent

Child

My friend _____ hurts me
when she says...

or when she...

Child

Three words that describe our family are...

Parent

Child

When I get scared about
something it is usually...

Child

What is one thing you wish
you could do better?

Parent

Child

I was really proud of you when you...

Parent

Child

Do you dream of being able to do something?

What would you do?

Child

What is your favorite subject? Who is your favorite teacher? Why?

Parent

Child

Why do you think it is important to save money?

What would you like to save money to buy?

Parent

Child

I will always remember the day you...

Parent

Child

Has anyone ever dared you to do something you knew you shouldn't do? What did you say?

Parent

Child

My favorite picture of us is...

because...

Parent

What is the best thing about being in our family? What is one thing you would change about our family if you could?

Parent

Child

Do you spend a lot of time wondering what your friends and other people think about you? Why or why not?

Parent

Child

What is the nicest thing you have ever done for someone?

Parent

Child

The best thing you ever did for me was...

Parent

Child

Do you ever dream of what it would be like to be someone else? Who do you dream of being like?

Parent

Child

What is the hardest thing about school this year?

What can I do to help?

Child

What do you think heaven will be like?

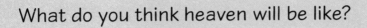

Parent

Child

I feel bad that I never told you...

Parent

Child

Do you know anyone who is really in need?

What can we do to help them?

Parent

Child

What is one thing you admire about each person in our family?

Parent

Child

I miss the way you use to...

Parent

Child

Which of your friends do you feel the most pressure from? Which do you feel the least pressure from?

Parent

Child

Name two of your strengths and two
of your weaknesses.

Parent

Child

The best present you ever gave me was...

Parent

Child

It makes me feel good when you tell me...

Parent

Child

If you could solve one problem in the world, what problem would you solve?

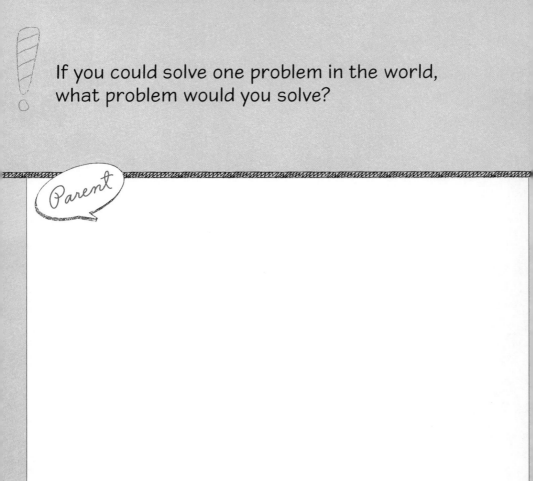

Parent

I trust you because...

Parent

Child

Who is the meanest kid at school?

Who is the nicest? Who needs a friend?

Parent

Child

What's your most treasured possession?

Why is it so special to you?

Parent

Child

How are we alike? How are we different?

Parent

Child

Have you ever been bullied?

If so, what did you do about it?

Parent

Child

What is the hardest thing about being in
a family and getting along with everyone?

Parent

Child

Have you ever been in a situation where you did not feel safe? What did you do?

Parent

Child

What is one mistake you have made that you would do differently given the chance? What would you do?

Parent

Child

You deserve an award for...

Parent

Child

I was really glad you were with me when...

Parent

If you could be one famous person,
who would you like to be?

Parent

Child

What job would you like to have
when you grow up?

Why?

Parent

Child

What was the worst thing that ever happened
to you? What helped you get through it?

Parent

Child

The funniest thing you ever did was...

Parent

Child

This year, I would like to
break the habit of...

Parent

Child

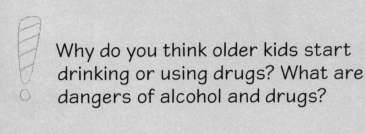

Why do you think older kids start drinking or using drugs? What are dangers of alcohol and drugs?

Parent

Child

What is your favorite family memory?

Why is it your favorite?

Child

What do you do when you feel lonely?
Disappointed? Stressed?

Parent

Child

My favorite holiday ever was...

because...

Parent

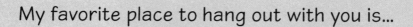

My favorite place to hang out with you is...

Parent

I was really proud of myself when I...

Parent

Child

When I daydream, it is usually about...

Parent

Child

What activity, sport, art project, or hobby would you like to try? Why does that look fun to you?

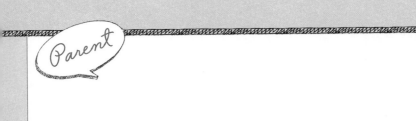

Parent

Child

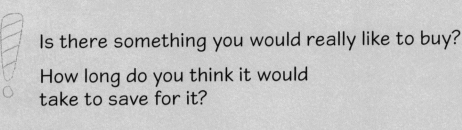

Is there something you would really like to buy?

How long do you think it would take to save for it?

Parent

Child

What is the most embarrassing thing
that has ever happened to you?

Parent

Child

I missed you when...

Child

What is your favorite book? Movie? Song? Why?

Parent

The greatest thing you ever taught me was...

Parent

What are the attributes of a good friend?

Do your friends have these attributes? Do you?

Parent

Child

Do you feel like I understand you? What do you
feel like I never really understand about you?

Parent

Child

If you had three wishes,
what would you wish for?

Parent

Child

I love to watch you...

Parent

Child

I am amazed at how much you know about...

Parent

I can't wait to...

some summer because...

Child

I wish we talked more about...

Parent

Child

What would you like to accomplish
this year in school?

Parent

Have you grown spiritually this year?

If so, how? If not, why?

Parent

Child

You were right about...

and I was wrong because...

Parent

Child

What makes you feel nervous?

Parent

Child

The best day of my life was...

The worst day of my life was...

Parent

Child

If you were stranded on an island, what three things would you want to have with you?

Parent

Child

Thank you for being kind to me when...

Parent

Child

Why should people give some of their money away to help others? Is there a ministry you would like to give to?

Parent

Child

The saddest thing I ever saw was...

Parent

Child

If you were an animal, you would be a...

because...

Parent

Child

Thank you for showing me how to...

Parent

Child

This week was really...

because...

What do you fight about most with each of your siblings? What can you do to change the situation?

Parent

Child

It is really hard for me to talk about...

because...

Parent

Child

What do you think makes you the happiest?

Parent

Child

My favorite compliment to receive is...

Parent

The most important person who ever lived is...

because...

Parent

Child

I am so grateful for the way you...

Parent

Child

The worst thing I ever saw someone do is...

Parent

Child

What do you like to do the most
with your siblings?

Why?

Parent

Child

Who do you like to talk to when you have a problem? Why did you choose that person?

Parent

The worst thing that ever
happened to me was...

Parent

Child

You make people happy when you...

Parent

One day I would like to help other people...

Parent

Child

What three things can I pray about
for you this year?

What can I do for you today?

Parent

Child

STAY
CONNECTED
Continue the journey to loving well.

CONNECT
with Mark

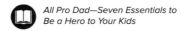 BLOG: www.markmerrill.com

facebook.com/markmerrill

READ
Mark's book

All Pro Dad—Seven Essentials to Be a Hero to Your Kids

CONNECT
with Susan

 BLOG: www.susan.me

facebook.com/susanmerrill

READ
Susan's book

The Passionate Mom—Dare to Parent in Today's World

Mark and Susan Merrill are the founders of Family First, a national non-profit organization. Explore our programs:

 All Pro Dad is a program to help dads love and lead their families well. We provide practical resources to dads through events in NFL and NCAA stadiums, our school chapter program, and online at allprodad.com.

 iMOM is a program to help moms love and nurture their families well. Being a mom is hard! We inspire and encourage moms to be the best they can be by providing resources that help online at imom.com.